WINNING THE WAR IN YOUR MIND

You Have What It Takes

Shannon U Frazier

RSI
PUBLISHING

Scriptures are taken from the English Standard Version of the Bible
Books may be ordered through booksellers or by contacting:
Shannon Frazier Ministries
www.afcbaytown.org
www.shannonfrazierministries.org

Raising the Standard International Publishing
Navarre, Florida
ISBN: 9781955830973
Printed in the United States of America
Edition Date: December 2022

DEDICATION

I want to dedicate this book to you. I wrote this book with you in mind. I genuinely believe that you can and will win in life. I believe you have what it takes, and inside you resides a true champion. I want you to discover all that you are by becoming who God created you to be. I consider myself an encourager, and I always encourage people to discover the best version of themselves and be that version for someone they may encounter. Thanks for reading this book, and I hope that it encourages you so much that you reach every goal and conquer every barrier that is stopping progress in your life!

Your Author,
Shannon

CONTENTS

-Introduction-

YOU HAVE WHAT IT TAKES

For years I struggled in my life, asking myself if I had what it took to be successful. I would often ask myself, will I ever be great? Will I ever have the ability to live a life of debt freedom? Will I be able to represent Jesus Christ effectively on earth? Will I ever be able to fulfill God's plan for my life?

I did not know exactly how it would happen or even if it would happen, but I knew deep down inside that it could happen. God began to speak to me, saying, "You have the authority to do exactly what needs to be done on this earth." In other words, He said to me, "Win the war in your mind. You have what it takes!" As a born-again Christian, I began believing God had given me exactly what I needed to succeed on this life journey! I just needed to win the war in my mind.

I believe you have what it takes because God has given you the talent, ability, and knowledge to live a successful life here on this earth. Success in the Kingdom of God does not mean that you are wealthy in finances but unhealthy in your physical body or that you are free from sickness and disease, but you carry a broken heart. Success in God's eyes is when

1

you run the race that God has already chartered out for you and you stay with it long enough to finish. The writer of Hebrews says this in Hebrews 12:1-3.

> *Hebrews 12:1-3 (ESV) Therefore, since we are surrounded by so great a cloud of witnesses, let us also lay aside every weight, and sin which clings so closely, and let us run with endurance the race that is set before us, 2 looking to Jesus, the founder and perfecter of our faith, who for the joy that was set before him endured the cross, despising the shame, and is seated at the right hand of the throne of God. 3 Consider him who endured from sinners such hostility against himself, so that you may not grow weary or fainthearted.*

"In other words, "You cannot quit"! God knows that you have been equipped to run this race, and you have the power living inside of you to not only run this race but to finish the race. God has fearfully and wonderfully made you, and nothing can harm or overtake you. Notice all throughout Scripture God said that all things are possible to those who can believe, and I believe that you and I are winners because we have been given free ability and free wisdom from God. Believing that you have what it takes is the key to receiving the greater things from God. Our mind is at strife with our Spirit and God's Spirit. We need to win the war in our minds. When God spoke to me and revealed that I had what it took, it changed my life and allowed me to view life differently. Have you ever noticed how it's easy to put things off and then regret that you didn't handle those things only to be faced with other critical situations, and you then become overwhelmed, and nothing gets done?

Life can be overwhelming when you look at it from a natural carnal sense. But the truth is, you have been given something great that is inside of every believer that will protect, lead, and navigate you through the pitfalls and snares of this life. Just remember, life in and of itself will not kill you. What will kill you is not knowing that you have what it takes to make it! Once I searched deep inside myself, asked myself hard questions, and faced shameful past experiences, I realized that I was reacting to adverse outcomes. I was allowing these past experiences to frustrate me, which resulted in procrastination becoming a part of my lifestyle. This realization explained why sadness, fear of failure, and high-stress levels were present in my life.

I was a regular Sunday morning church attendee, mostly playing the organ or piano in local church services every week. However, I was lost, depressed, and struggling with what success looked like. I didn't see anything working for me. Does this speak to you?

Every now and then, you need some insight and feedback to get your head in the right space, which can make a world of difference. I wrote this book to do just that. I want to give you the opportunity to challenge yourself and ask yourself the hard questions and get to the core of who you are. Why? Because once you begin to walk by faith and trust in God, that will unlock the one door you need to be opened. That is the door of possibility. I believe that as you read this book, you will know that you have been given what it takes to live the best life that you can live here on earth. You will not worry or doubt because you will know that God has already stamped the seal of "winner" on you! God spoke in His Word and said He wanted His will done here on earth like it is in Heaven. Remember, you must live in the now because yesterday is gone, and keep in mind that your best days are ahead because you have what it takes. I hope that you find this book uplifting and encouraging so that you get out of your stuck place. You will continue running the race that God has already planned for you to run.

-Chapter 1-

HOW DO YOU KNOW THAT YOU HAVE WHAT IT TAKES?

First and most importantly, you must recognize that the same God that made the earth, trees, fish, birds, moon, stars, and the sun is the same God that made you and me. The awesome part about it is that He didn't just make you any kind of way. He made you in His image and likeness.

> *Genesis 1:26-28 (ESV) Then God said, "Let us make man in our image, after our likeness. And let them have dominion over the fish of the sea and over the birds of the heavens and over the livestock and over all the earth and over every creeping thing that creeps on the earth." 27 So God created man in his own image, in the image of God he created him; male and female he created them. 28 And God blessed them. And God said to them, "Be fruitful and multiply and fill the earth and subdue it, and have dominion over the fish of the sea and over the birds of the heavens and over every living thing that moves on the earth."*

Isn't that awesome? God made you just like Him! He promised that your tongue would be a powerful weapon, and when you use His words with your tongue, it will produce greatness in your life! Jesus has qualified us as New Testament followers. Let's look at what the Apostle John tells us in 1 John 4:17-18.

> *1 John 4:17-18 (ESV) By this is love perfected with us, so that we may have confidence for the day of judgment, because as he is so also are we in this world. 18 There is no fear in love, but perfect love casts out fear. For fear has to do with punishment, and whoever fears has not been perfected in love.*

If we can remember the story of Abram in Genesis 15:1-8, God promised him that he would be the father of a son that would make Abram the Father of many nations.

> *Genesis 15:1-8 (ESV) After these things the word of the LORD came to Abram in a vision: "Fear not, Abram, I am your shield; your reward shall be very great." 2 But Abram said, "O Lord GOD, what will you give me, for I continue childless, and the heir of my house is Eliezer of Damascus?" 3 And Abram said, "Behold, you have given me no offspring, and a member of my household will be my heir." 4 And behold, the word of the LORD came to him: "This man shall not be your heir; your very*

own son shall be your heir." 5 And he brought him outside and said, "Look toward heaven, and number the stars, if you are able to number them." Then he said to him, "So shall your offspring be." 6 And he believed the LORD, and he counted it to him as righteousness. 7 And he said to him, "I am the LORD who brought you out from Ur of the Chaldeans to give you this land to possess." 8 But he said, "O Lord GOD, how am I to know that I shall possess it?"

Abram heard the words of God, and I can imagine that he evaluated himself. Through every evaluation, Abram always believed what God said and never wavered. He somehow managed to stay focused on the word spoken by God over his life. Abram found hope that God cut a blood covenant with him. The Father promised him with this covenant that the promise of a son would indeed happen for him.

Genesis 15:18 (ESV) On that day the LORD made a covenant with Abram, saying, "To your offspring I give this land, from the river of Egypt to the great river, the river Euphrates,

This blood covenant confirmed that God would fulfill His promises and gave Abram hope. It takes a covenant to provide you with hope, and Jesus came to this world to make a promise to us as an ultimate sacrifice because where there is no blood covenant, you become hopeless

> *Ephesians 2:12-13 (ESV) remember that you were at that time separated from Christ, alienated from the commonwealth of Israel and strangers to the covenants of promise, having no hope and without God in the world. 13 But now in Christ Jesus you who once were far off have been brought near by the blood of Christ.*

We have been given the ability and power to choose, and there comes a time in your life when you must determine whether you will *move with success* or *live in regret*. God gave you the ability to decide and to not only make a decision but to be able to act on the decisions that you make. Life is full of decisions, and God knew that it would be that way which is why He allows you to make the decision. If you never believe in yourself to decide to be great, don't count on anybody else to make that decision for you. Joshua said this in Joshua 24:15 as he recognized the power of daily decision-making.

> *Joshua 24:15 (ESV) And if it is evil in your eyes to serve the LORD, choose this day whom you will serve, whether the gods your fathers served in the region beyond the River, or the gods of the Amorites in whose land you dwell. But as for me and my house, we will serve the LORD."*

Joshua made a choice. He was very well aware of His options. Joshua chose one and stayed true to that choice. Even through the battles that Joshua faced, he remained focused on the choice that he made. God made you just like Him, and He said now, decide what you will do with this greatness. The option is yours. You have to determine if you will continue to sink or if you will no longer choose mediocrity as a way of life.

Great people are only great because they decide to be great. Winston Churchill said, "success is the ability to go from failure to failure without losing your enthusiasm." Decide today that no matter how far away you are from the finish line, you will reach that line, you will finish the race, and not only will you finish the race, but you will win if you make the right choice.

As believers, you are of God and come from the God class. You are one of His children. You are not great because of your ability, but you are great because of God's ability. God, Himself, decided to choose you. He placed you here today for such a time as this!

> *John 15:16 (ESV) You did not choose me, but I chose you and appointed you that you should go and bear fruit and that your fruit should abide, so that whatever you ask the Father in my name, he may give it to you.*

Esther 4:14 (ESV) For if you keep silent at this time, relief and deliverance will rise for the Jews from another place, but you and your father's house will perish. And who knows whether you have not come to the kingdom for such a time as this?"

Before you can move forward with this book, you must make a choice today. You must ask yourself this question right now, right where you are. The question is, "Am I willing to make the hard decision that will catapult me to my destiny?" If you are ever going to know that you have what it takes, it will derive from knowing what you are called to do and want to do. God sent you here with His plan, purpose, and resources to do the job. He has also given you His mind, His wisdom, and His ability. The Father will provide you with the provision you need for your vision.

You may have dreamed dreams and may have had many visions of yourself doing things that seemed impossible. You believe God has given you glimpses of His will for your life. However, maybe you have not allowed your natural mind to convince you that you cannot obtain what you envisioned. We call this stinking thinking. It is when you can't believe you will move out of the place of lack, poverty, brokenness, anxiety, and grief. You must believe that it's all up to you to decide to move forward or stay in your comfortable place. The Apostle Paul says this in 1 Corinthians 2:12, 16.

1 Corinthians 2:12 (ESV) Now we have received not the spirit of the world, but the Spirit who is from God, that we might understand the things freely given us by God.

1 Corinthians 2:16 (ESV) "For who has understood the mind of the Lord so as to instruct him?" But we have the mind of Christ.

I have learned over the years that God freely gives to us, but it is totally up to us to believe that God has also equipped us. Before I conclude this chapter, I want you to understand that when you discover what you are called to do and want to do and what that assignment is, you will also find your opposition. In other words, wherever your assignment is located, it is typically the same place where negativity, doubt, and fear are located. You cannot allow your opposing forces to override your ability to choose to keep moving forward. I often allowed my disappointment to stifle or stop my development for the assignment God had for me. Years of spiritual, mental, emotional, and relational growth were put on hold because of my perceptions about myself and my life. Don't allow the "inner you" to become the enemy in your life. As we move forward, you must realize that you have what it takes to be all God planned for you to be!

-Chapter 2-

YOU MUST SPEAK YOUR AUTHORITY

Y OU ARE God's representative on this earth. If you are a born-again believer, you have been given power and authority through Jesus Christ, and He has given you the ability to accomplish every task you will face. You must realize that a man shall be filled with the fruit of his words—whether good or evil. Proverbs 18:20-21 states this.

> *Proverbs 18:20-21 (ESV) From the fruit of a man's mouth his stomach is satisfied; he is satisfied by the yield of his lips. 21 Death and life are in the power of the tongue, and those who love it will eat its fruits.*

In other words, whatever you say is precisely what you will receive. Many believers have short-circuited the manifestation process by continually saying words that destroy the harvest that God has for them. I have learned that I must monitor what I say so that I don't postpone the manifestation process from happening immediately. I have served in many ministries over the years. I experienced believers who did not speak what God said and missed what God had already established and planned for their deliverance, salvation (sorteria), and even sanctification. We cannot allow our emotions to govern our speech. You will change your life when you take responsibility for your words. Judge your speech and train yourself only to speak what you believe. When you start to speak what you believe, you will create your world. If we never get in the Word of God and plant that Word in our hearts, we will never say what the Word says. Let's look at what our Lord spoke in Luke 6:45 concerning our confession.

Luke 6:45 (ESV) The good person out of the good treasure of his heart produces good, and the evil person out of his evil treasure produces evil, for out of the abundance of the heart his mouth speaks.

If you are a born-again believer, I want to suggest that you have the same creative ability as your Father. What you say flows from what is in your heart. The Scripture says that you have been given words from the Father to speak forth. Throughout the Bible, God spoke about the power of words and your tongue. God, the Father of Jesus, spoke, and things happened. Reading about how God framed the world with His words is amazing. In Genesis chapter 1, we see God saying let there be light, and the light overpowered the darkness.

13

> *Genesis 1:3-4 (ESV) And God said, "Let there be light," and there was light. 4 And God saw that the light was good. And God separated the light from the darkness.*

We see the Father speaking throughout Scripture, and things respond to His words. I know that this may be hard to understand, and you may be saying that you confessed and proclaimed some things in your life, and those things have never happened. In Genesis, we see God giving Adam the task of naming the animals.

> *Genesis 2:19 (ESV) Now out of the ground the LORD God had formed every beast of the field and every bird of the heavens and brought them to the man to see what he would call them. And whatever the man called every living creature, that was its name.*

For many years, I thought that was great because we saw the original man (ADAM) speaking and naming things on this earth. It wasn't that God could not name the animals with words, but I believe He was giving us a view of the power of our words. We have been given a mouth to speak, and we should recognize that and not take it for granted that we have power in our words.

In most cases, we only say what we believe. When you believe something, you will continuously speak about it repeatedly until you either get tired of saying it or until it becomes a reality in your life. For instance, have you told yourself that you would not have a bad day only to see a bad day in the making? What I am saying is this. You declared that you would not have a bad day, but when you stepped into your office that morning, you stepped right into the middle of chaos. You are now faced with a choice. Will you believe the positive declaration you started your day with, or will you accept the chaos you see? If you stick with your confession and believe that your words create your world, you will see that what you have spoken will come to life.

We must not believe what we see, but we must only believe what we say because it surely will happen when you use your mouth to speak it. When chaos is happening in the world, or things are not going right on the job or at home, we must believe in the power of our words. Primarily people with negative talk typically have negative lives. It all starts with what you say. I have a saying that goes something like this "What you say is what you get." You have to say exactly what the Word says, and you will see that Word come to life. The book of James talks about your tongue being like the rudder of a ship.

I want to submit to you today that your tongue steers your life in the same way that a rudder steers a ship. Even in high winds and storms on the sea, the rudder is powerful enough to steer the ship. In the same way, the tongue is powerful enough to steer your life. If you want to change the direction your life is headed, you must change the words you speak.

The Father has given us the ability to steer our lives by the promises of His Word. We must realize that our words are mighty. They are so powerful that God's Word says the small member of your body called the tongue can set great fires in your life.

James 3:4-6 (ESV) Look at the ships also: though they are so large and are driven by strong winds, they are guided by a very small rudder wherever the will of the pilot directs. 5 So also the tongue is a small member, yet it boasts of great things. How great a forest is set ablaze by such a small fire! 6 And the tongue is a fire, a world of unrighteousness. The tongue is set among our members, staining the whole body, setting on fire the entire course of life, and set on fire by hell.

God told you to speak to the unpleasant things in your life. He told you to command His hands to go to work in the area of lack in your life. He wants you to use your mouth to bring the results of Heaven into your life. When you believe your life can change because of your words, you will become serious about what flows from your lips. As a believer, you have been given the authority to speak and cause things to happen. If you are going to live on a level beyond mediocrity, you must be willing to say something that may not be visible to you, and it may not even be comfortable for you, but if you believe and say with your mouth what you want to create, it can happen for you. You will call that which is not as though it is. Abram was a man of faith who believed and hoped against hope.

> *Romans 4:17-18 (ESV) as it is written, "I have made you the father of many nations"—in the presence of the God in whom he believed, who gives life to the dead and calls into existence the things that do not exist. 18 In hope he believed against hope, that he should become the father of many nations, as he had been told, "So shall your offspring be."*

Understand that your mouth is creating things in your life right now that you may not even be aware of. Don't listen to the age-old cliché that says, "sticks and stones may break my bones, but words will never hurt me." Let me submit to you today that the wrong words can kill you! In my time of pastoring and leading people to Christ, I have discovered that when you speak words, they accomplish what you send them to do.

> *Isaiah 55:10-12 (ESV) "For as the rain and the snow come down from heaven and do not return there but water the earth, making it bring forth and sprout, giving seed to the sower and bread to the eater, 11 so shall my word be that goes out from my mouth; it shall not return to me empty, but it shall accomplish that which I purpose, and shall succeed in the thing for which I sent it. 12 "For you shall go out in joy and be led forth in peace; the mountains and*

17

the hills before you shall break forth into singing, and all the trees of the field shall clap their hands.

Remember, death and life are in the power of the tongue. Your tongue can be used as a force to propel your faith, or it can be your worst enemy if used incorrectly. Please understand that your mouth creates your world. It literally transcends you to the place of living above the world's way of speaking. Often the world will say that sarcasm and speaking idle words are alright or no big deal, but that is far from the truth. According to the Scriptures, every idle word will be accounted for. Let's look at Matthew 12:34-37 concerning our words.

Matthew 12:34-37 (ESV) You brood of vipers! How can you speak good, when you are evil? For out of the abundance of the heart the mouth speaks. 35 The good person out of his good treasure brings forth good, and the evil person out of his evil treasure brings forth evil. 36 I tell you, on the day of judgment people will give account for every careless word they speak, 37 for by your words you will be justified, and by your words you will be condemned."

When you understand that your words carry weight and steer your life, you will take what comes out of your mouth more seriously. What does the writer of Proverbs say?

Proverbs 30:32 (ESV) If you have been foolish, exalting yourself, or if you have been devising evil, put your hand on your mouth.

God knows the importance of your speech, and He doesn't want you perverting your speech with fruitless, idle words. Remember, you have what it takes!

-Chapter 3-

YOU MUST PRAY FOR YOUR AUTHORITY

We all have great needs and lots of desires in this life that drive us to pray, but most of the time, our pride blinds us to how needy we really are. We fall into seasons in our lives where there is very little or no prayer, especially if everything is going well. We tend to rely on habits and methods that we have learned to create a temporary solution or to help us feel as if we have solved our problems on our own. Most times, the average Christian will try everything else first. When nothing else works, and we are down to our last strand of strength, we say, "We've done all that we can do now; the only thing left to do is pray."

One of the main reasons people do not pray to God first is that many people feel it's not that bad or that they are not going to bother God with such a small problem. They say things like, "I'm not killing people," or "I'm not really a bad person." Those things are extremely deceiving and will lead you to a place of despair and self-pride. Praying is a very essential and critical form of communication with God. For the life of a believer, praying helps us build relationships and fellowship with the Father and fosters growth in our own lives.

I personally did not understand what it meant to pray. I thought that praying meant you would plead and beg God to give you the things you needed. After a season of pleading and begging, I thought you were then supposed to hope that God would do "some" of the stuff on that prayer list. After praying, I would often feel worse than I felt before I prayed. After all, I wasn't sure if God heard me or if He would help me because I knew the shortcomings in my life. The devil always made me look at my faults and performance. Therefore, I could never truly see what God had accomplished at the Cross of Calvary for me. At times I would even feel like this prayer just reminded me of how many problems I have in my life. As a result, my prayer life went from, sometimes, to every now and then, to never. As a believer, I often would skip prayer and block out all the bad occurrences in my life. I would tackle life without speaking to God, which frustrated and disappointed me because nothing seemed to work favorably.

My Christian life remained disappointing and frustrating until I really began to read the Word of God and saw for myself that the Father wanted me to have every promise in the Bible! He called me a winner and told me in the word that I was His chosen vessel, equipped to soar like an eagle and made to win. I was overwhelmed with joy when I read Scriptures like 2 Corinthians 1:19-20.

2 Corinthians 1:19-20 (ESV) For the Son of God, Jesus Christ, whom we proclaimed among you, Silvanus and Timothy and I, was not Yes and No, but in him it is always Yes. 20 For all the promises of God find their Yes in him. That is why it is through him that we utter our Amen to God for his glory.

Now it is God who makes both us and you stand firm in Christ. He anointed us, set His seal of ownership on us, and put His Spirit in our hearts as a deposit, guaranteeing what is to come. Isn't that great news? As I read that passage, I discovered that the word amen means "so be it," So every time I read something that God spoke in His Holy Word, I would add my amen or "so be it" to that promise! Hallelujah! I knew at that very moment that the words coming out of my mouth had to begin to line up with God's promises. We begin to see God's hand in operation when we pray boldly. His Hand was always there, but prayer opens our eyes to see what He has already completed for us. When you begin to pray with authority, you will see great things happen, like Elijah in 1 Kings 18:36-37.

1 Kings 18:36-37 (ESV) And at the time of the offering of the oblation, Elijah the prophet came near and said, "O LORD, God of Abraham, Isaac, and Israel, let it be known this day that you are God in Israel, and that I am your servant, and that I have done all these things at your word. 37 Answer me, O LORD, answer

*me, that this people may know that you, O
LORD, are God, and that you have turned their
hearts back."*

Elijah prayed with authority and, in doing so,
revealed to us that God wants us to command His
hands and pray with authority. The Lord sent him
into battle against the evil king Ahab and the 450
prophets of Baal. Let me explain. This event was a
spiritual battle that would show who was the real and
true God of Israel. Elijah used specific weapons such
as prayer and his knowledge of God's plan that was
revealed to him. He prayed with authority as a
prophet of God and allowed God to work through
him a miracle in the eyes of the people. Elijah
requested that Jehovah make Himself known as he
publicly voiced his cry to God before his opponents.
God heard his prayer and responded, and the people
declared, "The Lord, He is God." You see, when you
pray with authority and come to God boldly without
doubt or fear, you yield results.

*Mark 11:22-24 (ESV) And Jesus answered
them, "Have faith in God. 23 Truly, I say to you,
whoever says to this mountain, 'Be taken up
and thrown into the sea,' and does not doubt in
his heart, but believes that what he says will
come to pass, it will be done for him. 24
Therefore I tell you, whatever you ask in
prayer, believe that you have received it, and it
will be yours.*

23

Once you understand that God has given you everything you need and He is the source of your strength, you move from hopeful prayers to prayers of faith. Now, these prayers are what I consider to be prayers of faith! When you pray by faith, you must put your confidence and trust in the Word of God. These prayers are prayed from the Scripture and not from your words. For example, you take a Scripture passage and tell the Father, "Lord, You said in your Word that I am healed. According to 1 Peter 2:24, You said that by Your stripes I am healed, and I didn't have to hope that it would happen."

> *1 Peter 2:24 (ESV) He himself bore our sins in his body on the tree, that we might die to sin and live to righteousness. By his wounds you have been healed.*

I understood that I was given a promise, and God guaranteed this promise by His Word! Hallelujah! I want you to see that you never ever have to pray a defeated prayer or feel like you have to stress or worry if God will hear you. God made you a promise, and all that you have to do is pray in faith His promise, and it's a done deal! We have been given the power and right to communicate with our Father, and it is by what we call prayer. If we are ever going to get Elijah's results, we must pray with our God-given authority.

Prayer is a required discipline in the life of every believer because it authorizes God to get involved with your situation. The most powerful thing any person on this planet can do is pray. It doesn't mean you are the only person talking when you pray. Remember, you are in a conversation, meaning you speak and then listen because God wants to talk back to you. You have to fix your mind to focus on God and to expect to hear from Him. When you begin to commune with the Father, one of the first things you must do is give your full attention to hearing from Him. For example, Peter told a begging lame man to focus on him and John because he needed the man to fully concentrate on what he was asking.

> *Acts 3:1-5 (ESV) Now Peter and John were going up to the temple at the hour of prayer, the ninth hour. 2 And a man lame from birth was being carried, whom they laid daily at the gate of the temple that is called the Beautiful Gate to ask alms of those entering the temple. 3 Seeing Peter and John about to go into the temple, he asked to receive alms. 4 And Peter directed his gaze at him, as did John, and said, "Look at us." 5 And he fixed his attention on them, expecting to receive something from them.*

The man paid attention to Peter and John, expecting to receive something from them. He focused with expectation, obeyed, and received his healing. When you focus on this type of thinking, you will see God move in your life.

Acts 3:6-8 (ESV) But Peter said, "I have no silver and gold, but what I do have I give to you. In the name of Jesus Christ of Nazareth, rise up and walk!" 7 And he took him by the right hand and raised him up, and immediately his feet and ankles were made strong. 8 And leaping up, he stood and began to walk, and entered the temple with them, walking and leaping and praising God.

We have the ability to speak the Wisdom of God. Biblical wisdom is knowing what to do when we, in our own thinking, have no idea of where to start and what to do. God says that we speak hidden wisdom, and we have the ability to speak it out verbally. Let's look at what the Apostle Paul says in 1 Corinthians 2:6-7.

1 Corinthians 2:6-7 (ESV) Yet among the mature we do impart wisdom, although it is not a wisdom of this age or of the rulers of this age, who are doomed to pass away. 7 But we impart a secret and hidden wisdom of God, which God decreed before the ages for our glory.

You see that 2:7 says that what we are speaking will lift us into the **GLORY OF HIS PRESENCE**. So, when we speak the Word of God, we must understand that what we say will lift us into His presence. When we speak or pray in tongues, we speak wisdom in a mystery. In other words, when I speak in tongues, I'm uttering hidden wisdom, which is speaking wisdom in a mystery. When you speak in tongues, you really don't have any comprehension in your head as to what you are saying. You are simply yielding your tongue and language to Jesus by faith! When I read 1 Corinthians 14:2, it totally enlightened me. Let's take a look at this passage.

> *1 Corinthians 14:2 (ESV) For one who speaks in a tongue speaks not to men but to God; for no one understands him, but he utters mysteries in the Spirit.*

Praying in tongues is a prayer language that is the purest language that a person can speak. You are a tri-part (tripartite) being, meaning that you are a Spirit, live in a physical body, and have a soul. Understanding these three parts will help you know the reality of who you are.

Your soul is made up of your mind (how you think), will (how you choose), and your emotions (how you feel). When you pray from your mind, you are praying from an imperfect place, but when you pray from your spirit, you pray the most perfect prayer. This dynamic is because once you are saved and decide to make Christ your Lord and Savior, your spirit is born again and made NEW, and the Holy Spirit dwells in you. The Apostle Paul gives us the breakdown of the human being in 1 Thessalonians

5:23, along with the writer of the book of Hebrews in Hebrews 4:12.

> *1 Thessalonians 5:23 (ESV) Now may the God of peace himself sanctify you completely, and may your whole spirit and soul and body be kept blameless at the coming of our Lord Jesus Christ.*

> *Hebrews 4:12 (ESV) For the word of God is living and active, sharper than any two-edged sword, piercing to the division of soul and of spirit, of joints and of marrow, and discerning the thoughts and intentions of the heart.*

When you pray in tongues, you have prayed the most perfect prayer. Understand that you pray about things that you didn't know about. You pray what needs to be prayed and how it needs to be prayed in its most perfect form. Prayer is the key to removing the barriers or limitations in your life. So, continue to keep your communication open with God, and always remember that you have what it takes!!

-Chapter 4-

WALKING IN AUTHORITY

If you never ever walk in your God-given authority, you will never ever know the beauty of walking it out. God has given us the natural ability to walk here on this earth, and likewise, He has always referenced walking spiritually throughout the Bible. We see in Genesis 5:22 that Enoch walked with God.

Genesis 5:22 (ESV) Enoch walked with God after he fathered Methuselah 300 years and had other sons and daughters.

Walking with God was not unfamiliar to God's chosen people. Genesis 6:9 says this is the account of Noah and his family.

Genesis 6:9 (ESV) These are the generations of Noah. Noah was a righteous man, blameless in his generation. Noah walked with God.

We see that walking in the natural was mentioned throughout the bible. The Psalmist writes in Psalm 23:4 that while walking through the trials and tribulations of life, we should never be afraid.

Psalms 23:4 (ESV) Even though I walk through the valley of the shadow of death, I will fear no evil, for you are with me; your rod and your staff, they comfort me.

Isn't that great news!!!! As I walk through this journey called life, I am secure knowing that God has blessed me with every Spiritual blessing in Heavenly places, Praise God!! The word "walk" in Webster's dictionary means to move at a regular and fairly slow pace by lifting and setting down each foot in turn, never having both feet on or off the ground at once. As we move forward in our natural state by faith, it symbolizes what has already happened in a supernatural place. I'm saying what the Apostle Paul said in 2 Corinthians 5:7. We walk by faith, not sight!

2 Corinthians 5:7 (ESV) for we walk by faith, not by sight.

Faith is nothing more than placing your trust, belief, and confidence in the Word of God. You see, walking in authority is all about trusting, believing, and having confidence that God has given you the ability to do and accomplish the things that God spoke to you.

When you believe you have what it takes, you are learning to win the war in your mind. When you believe you have what it takes to create a better life for yourself and your family, a better career, or even a better attitude, you will get up like the man lying at the pool of Bethesda in John chapter 5. You will pick up your mat and walk into the newness of life!!

> *John 5:8-11 (ESV) Jesus said to him, "Get up, take up your bed, and walk." 9 And at once the man was healed, and he took up his bed and walked. Now that day was the Sabbath. 10 So the Jews said to the man who had been healed, "It is the Sabbath, and it is not lawful for you to take up your bed." 11 But he answered them, "The man who healed me, that man said to me, 'Take up your bed, and walk.'"*

Often times you will have to walk away from negative situations that try and destroy your peace and what God placed inside of you. Remember that God wants you to walk into your wealthy, healthy place knowing you are blessed. You can now confidently step out into this world and witness to others about the goodness of Jesus!

I remember a time in my life when I walked into my calling as a Pastor. It seemed to be one of the most frightening times in my life. I stepped out on faith into an area I was totally unfamiliar with and trusted God. I have a very vivid picture of this day in my mind. I remember sitting at home in my office and wondering how I would complete the mission and will of God for my life. While sitting there, God spoke to me very clearly and said, "Go to your local barbershop where you take your sons to get their haircut and drop off a CD of one of your sermons." I thought at first it was a great idea until it was time to move. I began to have negative thoughts like, "They will never listen to my CD," or thoughts like, "It's just a waste of time."

I finally got out of my office and headed to the barbershop, only to get to the shop and say, "This is just stupid." Doubt set in, and I began to say repeatedly that nobody blows their own horn by arrogantly walking into a place and saying here, take and listen to me preaching. I was like, no, that's not going to work. Finally, I just rushed into the shop and placed the CD in the hands of the barber and told him that it was my CD, and I immediately turned around and walked briskly straight out of the door. To my surprise, I walked in on the next barber visit, and they were listening to my CD. The barber told me that a Pastor wanted to meet me. I called the Pastor, and this man submitted to helping me establish my ministry. I couldn't believe it! It was amazing! I trusted what God spoke by walking into the place of destiny.

Having a religious mindset doesn't mean we are aligned with God's Word, and it is just as dangerous as walking in the flesh. This event caused me to research the definition of religion. What I discovered completely shocked me. The word "religion" is a specific fundamental set of beliefs and practices generally agreed upon by a number of persons or sections. Religion says you must put up with whatever the Devil throws at you. Religion causes us to adopt and sing songs like "I'm coming up on the rough side of the mountain" and "I'm

32

doing my best to make it in." These are not "overcomer" songs but songs giving the impression we are victims just surviving.

As I studied and meditated on this definition of religion, I wondered what the word Christianity meant because I hoped there would be a difference between religion and Christianity. And I was right. The definition of Christianity is a Christ-like belief, practice, or attitude. Notice the distinct differences between the two. Religion is man-made beliefs agreed on by several people, whereas Christianity is believing and being in one accord with Jesus and what He said. If you are going to walk in authority, move away from the crowd and opinions of people and believe what Jesus has accomplished. When you understand that Jesus accomplished his mission because He kept walking towards that hill called Calvary, He kept moving and never once stopped to complain. Our Lord accomplished this mission so that you and I could have what it takes to live an abundant life full of grace, love, joy, and hope in this world. Keep walking in the direction God tells you because if He is with you, you have what it takes!

-Chapter 5-

IT'S UP TO YOU

There are two systems in operation in this world. One is the world system, and the other is the Kingdom of God. The world's system functions by fear and intimidation, and that system seems to flourish or produce results. However, it is filled with hate, jealousy, and competition, leading to various health issues, including mental problems.

The other system is the Kingdom of God, which functions by God's love. The love in this system is what moves this system and supplies this system and every person attached to it. The love of God is the distinguishing mark in this system because it is the only way the world will recognize you as a disciple.

> *John 13:34-35 (ESV) A new commandment I give to you, that you love one another: just as I have loved you, you also are to love one another. 35 By this all people will know that you are my disciples, if you have love for one another."*

The Father gives us choices as to who we will serve.

Joshua 24:14-15 (ESV) "Now therefore fear the LORD and serve him in sincerity and in faithfulness. Put away the gods that your fathers served beyond the River and in Egypt, and serve the LORD. 15 And if it is evil in your eyes to serve the LORD, choose this day whom you will serve, whether the gods your fathers served in the region beyond the River, or the gods of the Amorites in whose land you dwell. But as for me and my house, we will serve the LORD."

To operate and function in the Kingdom of God and see the manifestation, or shall I say the fruit of this Kingdom, is going to be totally up to you. I believe you have what it takes. The Father has given you His ability to love and to create a loving environment. But again, it is up to you to decide to divorce or let go of habits that reveal or lead you to a place of destruction. I have often held on to stinking thinking and habits from the world system, even though I desired to operate and yield Godly results.

We all know that you reap what you sow, which is a natural law of the universe, and that law has remained to be true since the beginning of time. If you take the time to sow apple seeds, you will reap apples. However, if oranges come into harvest from an apple tree, we have a serious problem. Here is the reality. You have been given a choice to live a life that will yield much fruit and great results, but the choice is yours, not God's, and certainly not the devil's. It is totally and unequivocally up to you. When you know that you can choose to be sad, jealous, or even hurt, you will make the decision that will work in your favor. The Apostle Paul teaches in Ephesians 4:22-24 that you must put on the new and take off the old. You must establish your day and what will be your life's outcome by your choices.

> *Ephesians 4:22-24 (ESV) to put off your old self, which belongs to your former manner of life and is corrupt through deceitful desires, 23 and to be renewed in the spirit of your minds, 24 and to put on the new self, created after the likeness of God in true righteousness and holiness.*

God has already prepared you for the journey ahead, but you must take the opportunities that God presents and be willing to soar and fly. Most people fail because of a lack of determination. Ludwig Beethoven was five years old when he played the violin masterfully, and at the age of thirteen, this prodigy in music was an accomplished pianist. By the age of twenty, he had studied under Mozart and Haydn. He had written nine symphonies, but he began losing his hearing, and by the age of fifty, he was completely deaf. Beethoven was determined to get the music out that was inside of him. So, what he did was take the legs of the piano off, place the piano on the floor, and lay beside the piano so that he could feel the vibrations of the music through the floor.

Through this technique, Ludwig Beethoven wrote his greatest symphonies when he was completely deaf through pure determination. One day they heard him pounding with his fist on the piano, screaming these words, "I will take life by the throat, I will not let life defeat me, I will win."

As I have stated repeatedly in this chapter, it's up to you! Every day your life is built on a decision. It is a decision to get up and walk or to lie down and cry. Your choices in this life can align you with what God has already done for you, or they can take you down a road that leads to destruction. The Word of God tells us that there is a way that seems right but ends in destruction.

> *Proverbs 14:12 (ESV) There is a way that seems right to a man, but its end is the way to death.*

David, the man after God's own heart, lost his family at Ziglag. He asked God what he should do, and God said to pursue. Now one thing that I know about God is if the Father tells you to go after something, that means He plans on you getting it. He doesn't tell you to go after it and pursue it so that He can tease you with failure. I know that God has told you to pursue a dream, to pursue an impossible task in your life, but it's up to you to decide to get it done. You will have what you say when you abide in what God has already said, and the Word abides in you.

I know we talked about words in a previous chapter, but I want you to understand that you have what you say! That seems so farfetched for many people because it seems like whatever will happen will be what will happen, or we say things like, "If it's meant to be, then it will happen for me." This type of talk or thinking is far from the truth. I have realized that it's up to you to say what God has said about you. I have decided in my own life that if my words are going to carry the weight to change my situation, then I'd better get the right words out of my mouth. I had to remember that it was up to me to learn the correct words to say, and it would be up to me to speak them. See, if you say what God has already said, you will see what He has already completed for your life. I remember reading that Jesus only said what He heard His Father say, and He had major results.

> *John 5:19 (ESV) So Jesus said to them, "Truly, truly, I say to you, the Son can do nothing of his own accord, but only what he sees the Father doing. For whatever the Father does, that the Son does likewise.*

> *John 12:49 (ESV) For I have not spoken on my own authority, but the Father who sent me has himself given me a commandment—what to say and what to speak.*

> *John 14:10-12 (ESV) Do you not believe that I am in the Father and the Father is in me? The*

words that I say to you I do not speak on my own authority, but the Father who dwells in me does his works. 11 Believe me that I am in the Father and the Father is in me, or else believe on account of the works themselves. 12 "Truly, truly, I say to you, whoever believes in me will also do the works that I do; and greater works than these will he do, because I am going to the Father.

After it's all said and done, it's up to you to put these words in your heart because whatever you have inside of you will come out of your mouth. You have what it takes! It's up to you.

-Chapter 6-

YOU MUST BE WILLING TO EMBRACE YOUR IDENTITY IN CHRIST

Often times we are all right with the "status quo" of what we consider to be a normal life. Because we are creatures of habit, we tend to repeat patterns and cycles. When you understand that your identity is very important to the Kingdom of God, you will search to find out who you are. Many people walk around establishing themselves and identifying their lives with external things like jobs, cars, or clothes. But these things cannot create your identity. Your identity in Christ can no longer be the same. Your new standard is now a life of dependency on Christ. Galatians 2:20 says I have been crucified with Christ. Then whose life lives in and through me?

Galatians 2:20 (ESV) I have been crucified with Christ. It is no longer I who live, but Christ who lives in me. And the life I now live in the flesh I live by faith in the Son of God, who loved me and gave himself for me.

40

I have discovered that the world is changing, and a "new normal" is the topic of discussion. There are many trendy topics and ideas invading schools, homes, and jobs. Though some are very intriguing, these new ideas are not God's ideas or God-inspired. The new culture being created with these ideologies will try to persuade you to conform or never change and just be who you are. The new normal says that anything goes, and basically, you answer to yourself in many instances.

I believe the cultural shift in America is because of an identity crisis in people. When you decide to come to Christ and believe in what He has done for you, there will be an overwhelming thought that this is too good to be true because of the immense love and life that comes to you. If I were to ask you, "Do you know who you are?" Your immediate answer would probably be, "Of course, I know who I am" But can you imagine what it would be like if suddenly you lost all memory of your name, had no idea of where you lived, no longer recognized who your family members were, and you could not remember where you worked? It would be catastrophic, to say the least. There is an enormous place of security in knowing who you are. That is the reason we, as creatures of habit, fight and condemn change.

People are secure in what they know, especially if there are not many facts about the outcome of a change. In the lives of believers, that metamorphosis or transformation occurred at the moment of excepting Christ into their lives. We use a

41

term called "Born Again." The phrase "born again" literally means "born from above." A biblical character named Nicodemus had a real need, he needed a change of his heart—a spiritual transformation, and he wanted to know how to truly change His life. We read about this event in John 3:1-7

> *John 3:1-7 (ESV) Now there was a man of the Pharisees named Nicodemus, a ruler of the Jews. 2 This man came to Jesus by night and said to him, "Rabbi, we know that you are a teacher come from God, for no one can do these signs that you do unless God is with him." 3 Jesus answered him, "Truly, truly, I say to you, unless one is born again he cannot see the kingdom of God." 4 Nicodemus said to him, "How can a man be born when he is old? Can he enter a second time into his mother's womb and be born?" 5 Jesus answered, "Truly, truly, I say to you, unless one is born of water and the Spirit, he cannot enter the kingdom of God. 6 That which is born of the flesh is flesh, and that which is born of the Spirit is spirit. 7 Do not marvel that I said to you, 'You must be born again.'*

Jesus simply said to Nicodemus that he must establish a new normal, realizing that he had a Father in heaven. Jesus was challenging Nicodemus's natural understanding and asking Him to embrace something He could not physically or naturally see. Your identity in Christ has to become your new normal.

When you are "Born Again," this simply means that the old is gone and the new is here. Your Spirit has been made brand new. The day you made Jesus the Lord of your life, He impacted your Spirit man; the old you died, and the new you, the "New Creation," was born again.

Jesus died and rose again so we could be adopted into a family that gives life and love freely and abundantly. If you are going to experience this new normal, you will have to embrace the facts about who Christ says you are. The Apostle Paul addresses this in Ephesians 1:7-10.

> *Ephesians 1:7-10 (ESV) In him we have redemption through his blood, the forgiveness of our trespasses, according to the riches of his grace, 8 which he lavished upon us, in all wisdom and insight 9 making known to us the mystery of his will, according to his purpose, which he set forth in Christ 10 as a plan for the fullness of time, to unite all things in him, things in heaven and things on earth.*

Wow, this is awesome news! God has called each and every believer to a place of freedom. When you really begin to peel back the reality of who God is and find out where you are in the equation and the part you must play, you will experience freedom like never before. However, with that freedom comes responsibility and obedience. God is calling you to obey Him at any cost. If we are going to move and progress in this "New Normal," we must not continue to walk in ignorance or lack of knowledge in certain areas. I read this Scripture, which literally challenged my thinking in certain areas of my life.

> *Acts 17:30-31 (ESV) The times of ignorance God overlooked, but now he commands all people everywhere to repent, 31 because he has fixed a day on which he will judge the world in righteousness by a man whom he has appointed; and of this he has given assurance to all by raising him from the dead."*

We can all live radically changed lives. All that is required is obedience to God, a willingness to think differently, and a desire to grow spiritually. There are levels of maturity, and God expects us to prosper in every area of our lives. He also expects us to move out of fear and into faith, which is a place that does not operate from a sense, knowledge, or reason realm. He wants us to do this from a position of faith and obedience to Him. In other words, God wants us to hear His Word and do it without wavering.

Many people think that being radical is some crazy person that runs around disputing certain laws and principles, but that's not it at all. Being radical simply means that you are not afraid of the past because you are focused solely on the promises in God's Word for your future. Radical believers understand that the *New Normal* calls for bold people who find the Word of God as the final authority in their lives. You must be willing to deny yourself praise from others because when that doesn't happen, you may question whether you have what it takes. You cannot continue putting energy in places with very little return. This principle may sound selfish, but God has called His children to produce, multiply, and bear fruit. The New Normal is upon us, so we must respond by being willing to step into a place where all of our certainties rest on the truth of the Gospel of Jesus! This powerful truth will change your life and the way that you think.

Always know and remember, "you have what it takes!"

-Chapter 7-

YOU MUST BE WILLING TO STAY FOCUSED

W hat difference would it make in how you accepted what is happening in your life right now if you saw it as an opportunity to know Jesus Christ more personally? The problems or crises you may face can be seen as an opportunity. Knowing Jesus involves experiencing His resurrection power which means that some things in our lives have to die. To gain in Christ is to lose our life in Him. When you really know Jesus, it involves experiencing the power of His resurrection. It also involves understanding the fellowship of His sufferings.

Philippians 3:8-11 (ESV) Indeed, I count everything as loss because of the surpassing worth of knowing Christ Jesus my Lord. For his sake I have suffered the loss of all things and count them as rubbish, in order that I may gain Christ 9 and be found in him, not having a righteousness of my own that comes from the law, but that which comes through faith in Christ, the righteousness from God that depends on faith— 10 that I may know him and the power of his resurrection, and may share

*his sufferings, becoming like him in his death,
11 that by any means possible I may attain the
resurrection from the dead.*

*1 Peter 2:20-25 (ESV) For what credit is it if,
when you sin and are beaten for it, you
endure? But if when you do good and suffer for
it you endure, this is a gracious thing in the
sight of God. 21 For to this you have been
called, because Christ also suffered for you,
leaving you an example, so that you might
follow in his steps. 22 He committed no sin,
neither was deceit found in his mouth. 23
When he was reviled, he did not revile in
return; when he suffered, he did not threaten,
but continued entrusting himself to him who
judges justly. 24 He himself bore our sins in his
body on the tree, that we might die to sin and
live to righteousness. By his wounds you have
been healed. 25 For you were straying like
sheep, but have now returned to the Shepherd
and Overseer of your souls.*

We share in His sufferings as we die to
ourselves and live for Him. In this, we give up what
we want and serve others for a greater purpose, just
as he did in his suffering and death. It will take focus
for you to become a follower of Jesus because you will
have to deny yourself from feeling the urge to quit
when things begin to be uncomfortable for you.

I remember reading about a man named Paul
in the Bible. Paul did not doubt that he knew he

would rise again. He knew that nothing could ever separate him from God's love.

> *Romans 8:37-39 (ESV) No, in all these things we are more than conquerors through him who loved us. 38 For I am sure that neither death nor life, nor angels nor rulers, nor things present nor things to come, nor powers, 39 nor height nor depth, nor anything else in all creation, will be able to separate us from the love of God in Christ Jesus our Lord.*

You see, Paul was focused on the love of God and understood that nothing could separate him from that love. Paul knew and understood that we are responsible for putting intense effort, focus, and time into following Jesus. There are many things involved in striving, reaching out, or exerting sincere effort to come to know Jesus. Answer these questions before you leave this chapter. What are you focused on? Are you focused on past achievements or past failures? Or both? After you answer those questions, honestly listen to this. If you are focused anywhere but on the goal ahead, you will not exert the effort needed to achieve it. When your focus is behind you, you typically lose sight of what is coming to you. Paul realized that he had not arrived and only one option was open for him. Paul knew he had to press on.

There is no turning back when your eyes are focused on what is ahead. Paul was focused on one thing and would not let those things behind him distract him. He pressed on for the prize.

> *Philippians 3:12-14 (ESV) Not that I have already obtained this or am already perfect, but I press on to make it my own, because Christ Jesus has made me his own. 13 Brothers, I do not consider that I have made it my own. But one thing I do: forgetting what lies behind and straining forward to what lies ahead, 14 I press on toward the goal for the prize of the upward call of God in Christ Jesus.*

There is a deception to live either in the past or in the future. The Father wants us to press on in the present because the present is where eternity touches us now. Paul knew that a race is won only in the present moment, not in the past or the future. He knew and understood that it was a high calling to press on toward the mark because it was so much above the ideas of men. Paul knew pressing on in the present would summon us to where Christ sits at the right hand of God.

The most powerful thing that you can do as a Christian is to not go back to old thoughts and actions but to keep your mind focused on what God is doing now. When God makes you whole, you must focus on that and not allow Satan to rob you. As a believer, you need to know how to win in life, and focusing on the goal is the best way to obtain success. I always say that you keep the main thing the main thing which simply means staying focused on the destination and does not quit!

Realize there is an anointing designed for conquering, and it is available to you. But to tap into it, you must know that you cannot bypass or skip the steps it will take you to get to the destination. One of the most critical steps in this process is to focus on the vision or goal ahead. You must possess a winning attitude and know you will win every battle you face. To do this, your focus must be unwavering, and your mind must be fixed on the prize.

In Philippians 3:12-14 we see that Paul understood consistent conquest has its roots in God. When you are rooted in God, you can run the race He has called you to run and not be distracted by anything outside of that race that He has built for you. Always know that you have what it takes, and when you apply the things of God in your life, you will see the fruit of His Blessing as a great reward.

-Chapter 8-

YOU MUST BE WILLING TO REST

N ow once you have fixed your mind on the goal and know where you are going and what you will do, you must now find your rest in Jesus. Resting in Jesus is not a very easy task. When you focus and make up your mind to rest in our Lord Jesus Christ, you take the stress of the world off your shoulders; you cast that burden on Jesus. The Apostle Peter tells us this in 1 Peter 5:6-7.

1 Peter 5:6-7 (ESV) Humble yourselves, therefore, under the mighty hand of God so that at the proper time he may exalt you, 7 casting all your anxieties on him, because he cares for you.

As followers of Jesus, we have not been granted immunity from life's storms, but we have been given a choice on how we respond in and through the storm. Noah was not delivered from the storm but through the storm. Daniel was not delivered from the trial of the lion's den. He was delivered in the lion's den. If you get bad news and it takes you to a place of high anxiety or stress, you have to remember that resting in the finished work of

Jesus is having total trust and complete reliability in God.

My confidence in the Lord Jesus Christ is founded on what He accomplished for me at the Cross, and this must be my standard of victory! Basically, having confidence that I don't have to worry because my God has supplied me with the ability to rest on His promise is where I find rest. If you have no confidence in what Jesus has done for you, you will not be able to enter this glorious rest. You see, confidence becomes the strength to help me to enter this rest, and as a follower of Jesus, my confidence comes when I know that I am working on my mind. The Word of God must be allowed to renew my mind, as the Apostle Paul tells us in Romans 12:1-2.

> *Romans 12:1-2 (ESV) I appeal to you therefore, brothers, by the mercies of God, to present your bodies as a living sacrifice, holy and acceptable to God, which is your spiritual worship. 2 Do not be conformed to this world, but be transformed by the renewal of your mind, that by testing you may discern what is the will of God, what is good and acceptable and perfect.*

I must renew my mind daily. To gain the confidence needed to renew your mind, there must be rest in the *Good News* of Jesus. The *Good News* says it's finished. It is already done! Here This! It is finished! When I renew my mind, I take my thoughts,

ideas, and philosophies captive and exchange them
for God's thoughts and His ideas.

*2 Corinthians 10:4-5 (ESV) For the weapons of
our warfare are not of the flesh but have divine
power to destroy strongholds. 5 We destroy
arguments and every lofty opinion raised
against the knowledge of God, and take every
thought captive to obey Christ,*

In everything you deal with in life, you have to
ask yourself the question, what does the word think
or say about this situation or that circumstance? Take
that word of God and allow that word to hold final
authority in your life. Now renewing the mind is an
everyday life process. If you are going to rest in Jesus,
you must confess God's Word for yourself. The reality
is that *LIFE BRINGS BAGGAGE*. The longer you live,
the more you have to pick up, and if you don't learn
how to cast it off of you, you'll begin to get numb to
love, mood swings, snapping at people, bad attitudes,
and evil speech towards people. People cannot figure
out what is wrong with them because they are
burdened with stress and the inability to rest. When
you get tired of dealing with life issues, it is a
guarantee that Christ will be there with you! Learn to
cast those cares on Him. Christ is always standing
with open arms telling you and me to rest. To obtain
the rest God has for you, you must be willing to come
to Him and learn to abide in Him. Let's take a good
look at our Lord's words in Matthew 11:28-30.

Matthew 11:28-30 (ESV) Come to me, all who labor and are heavy laden, and I will give you rest. 29 Take my yoke upon you, and learn from me, for I am gentle and lowly in heart, and you will find rest for your souls. 30 For my yoke is easy, and my burden is light."

Now let's take a moment to understand that resting in Jesus Christ does not mean that we will fall asleep. It is not an absence of activity. Rest in the Kingdom of God is the *"REST"* that the Father promises us in Him. Understand this. Our rest is not found in a day but in the person of our Lord Jesus Christ. This rest brings participation in and enjoyment of the blessing that He has planned for you! This rest is an assurance that God has already completed the task for me, and my part is to obey His leadership by faith. Here is a reality. If you are seriously living that Christian life, you will face challenges, tests, and trials. In fact, the godlier you become, the more disciplined to the vision and assignment the Father will give you.

It sometimes seems difficult to focus on prayer or even rest in the finished work of the Cross because the devil does not want you to focus and enter this rest. There is a rest that you and I have been called to. Let's look at what the writer of Hebrews says in Hebrews 4:5-11. Take a good look at 4:9.

Hebrews 4:5-11 (ESV) And again in this passage he said, "They shall not enter my rest." 6 Since therefore it remains for some to enter it, and those who formerly received the good news failed to enter because of disobedience, 7 again he appoints a certain day, "Today," saying through David so long afterward, in the words already quoted, "Today, if you hear his voice, do not harden your hearts." 8 For if Joshua had given them rest, God would not have spoken of another day later on. 9 So then, there remains a Sabbath rest for the people of God, 10 for whoever has entered God's rest has also rested from his works as God did from his. 11 Let us therefore strive to enter that rest, so that no one may fall by the same sort of disobedience.

Jesus desires for you and me to rest in Him because He won the battle at Calvary's cross for us. The devil wants to pressure you so that you continue to stress and never consider entering into the rest of God. If you follow the route of comfortability and least resistance, you will fail to enter into the rest of God, where His promises reside. The reality is that your salvation may be secure in Heaven. However, your inheritance here on this earth may be squandered, and the devourer (better known as the enemy) can and will consume everything that Jesus provided for you if you allow it.

The Cross of our Lord Jesus Christ provides the place where you will find love, peace, joy, and rest. The Hebrew word translated as "rest" means "to be at peace," "to be still," and "to be quiet or calm." In the place of "the rest in the Lord," some Bible translations say, "Be still before the Lord" (ESV and NIV), "Be silent before the Lord" (CSB), "Surrender yourself to the Lord" (GW), and "Be still in the presence of the Lord" (NLT). These different statements suggest that one must dwell in the presence of the Lord and surrender to His Lordship. Jesus has called us to rest, and that rest will always produce. Recognize that you have what it takes because of your ability to rest in Him.

-Chapter 9-

YOU MUST RECOGNIZE THE POWER OF THE CROSS

There is power wonder-working power in the Blood of The Lamb! When you experience being born from above, born anew, born again, you must enter the reality that your life is blessed, and you can experience the wonderful work of Jesus and the cross! The Cross of Jesus carried so much weight for mankind because it enabled us to have eternal life. That eternal life should be experienced every day right here on earth. When Jesus was beaten, tormented, and nailed to the cross, blood poured from His head down to His feet. This blood flowing over His entire body represents how God designed us to partake in the Power that has been delivered to us. It represents a unique aspect of our deliverance.

Many points of victory give us the understanding that we have complete redemption and triumph over any satanic oppression or stronghold. The Cross that Jesus carried is, in my opinion, an intersection where we get to experience and witness a natural man who, while He walked on the earth, prayed prayers that said God, not my will be done, but your will be done in my life. Yet we see this man humble Himself, drop His head, and die on the cross for a sinner like me. That's enough to stop and ask the question, why? Why would someone die for me? Why would He risk His fame and fortune that He had for someone who doesn't really love Him? Well, this Cross gives us insight into why and helps us to understand that Jesus loves you and me, so much so that He paid the price with His life so that you could be free to carry out the assignment that God purposed you and me to carry. Jesus took away our sins and placed them upon Himself at the cross, satisfying God's justice. Jesus' death made it possible for fallen man to have peace with God, as the Apostle Paul stated in 2 Corinthians 5:18-21.

> *2 Corinthians 5:18-21 (ESV) All this is from God, who through Christ reconciled us to himself and gave us the ministry of reconciliation; 19 that is, in Christ God was reconciling the world to himself, not counting their trespasses against them, and entrusting to us the message of reconciliation. 20 Therefore, we are ambassadors for Christ, God making his appeal through us. We implore you on behalf of Christ, be reconciled to God. 21 For our sake he made him to be sin who knew no sin, so that in him we might become the righteousness of God.*

The word "reconcile" means to restore friendly relations between people that were separated. This reconciliation is what the Power of the Cross did for you and me. It restored friendly relations between God and fallen man. As a born-again believer, your righteousness and justification in Christ can be accepted because you know God is your friend! *That's good news!!* When we see that we have a great relationship with God, it places us in a good, pleasant mindset and will help us to focus on our purpose. The Apostle John's love for our Lord was apparent, as was our Lord's love for John. Read what our Lord spoke in John 15:15 just hours before His time in the garden and His arrest.

> *John 15:14-15 (ESV) You are my friends if you do what I command you. 15 No longer do I call you servants, for the servant does not know what his master is doing; but I have called you friends, for all that I have heard from my Father I have made known to you.*

You have what it takes to walk in your purpose and pass through the storms of life! The Power of the Cross at Calvary, where Jesus hung, bled, and died, was the place that started our reconciliation! Oh, but it didn't stop there. The Cross may have seemed to be the ending place and the place of failure. It seemed to be the end, but Jesus made us a promise! He told the Pharisees that if they destroyed this temple in three days, He would raise it up, which is precisely what happened three days later!

John 2:18-22 (ESV) So the Jews said to him, "What sign do you show us for doing these things?" 19 Jesus answered them, "Destroy this temple, and in three days I will raise it up." 20 The Jews then said, "It has taken forty-six years to build this temple, and will you raise it up in three days?" 21 But he was speaking about the temple of his body. 22 When therefore he was raised from the dead, his disciples remembered that he had said this, and they believed the Scripture and the word that Jesus had spoken.

The Jews thought Jesus was talking about a physical building that would be raised, but He spoke about His own crucifixion and resurrection. He knew that these Pharisees and Sadducees were ignorant of who He was because they knew and kept the Law written in the Torah, but they did not know the Messiah. Jesus rose! He got up from that grave, and because of that, He placed resurrection power in you and me.

The power of that Cross brought us freedom, joy, life, strength, and success! You have what it takes to walk in your God-given plan and destiny! Jesus made the impossible very possible for every believer. The power of the Cross and the Word of God will help you in the war in your mind. We all fight with stinking thinking. The moment that you change your thinking and surrender to the process that God has for you is the moment that you change your life! There is a song written by Lewis E. Jones that says there is power, power, wonder-working power in the Precious Blood of the Lamb. Hallelujah! That blood was shed at the Cross for you and me so we can live this life on earth pleasing to the Father! You have been given the ability to overcome every hardship and go through every storm. I do not doubt in my mind that you have what it takes!

You have what it takes to walk in your God-given plan and destiny! Jesus made the possible for every believer. The moment that you change your thinking and surrender to the process that God has for you is the moment that you

-Chapter 10-

YOU ARE A WINNER

It's an awesome experience to know that God chose us to win in life! Those who belong to God, obey His Word, and live in obedience to what He spoke about will experience the best of the best. The prophet Isaiah proclaimed this concerning our sins.

> *Isaiah 1:18-20 (ESV) "Come now, let us reason together, says the LORD: though your sins are like scarlet, they shall be as white as snow; though they are red like crimson, they shall become like wool. 19 If you are willing and obedient, you shall eat the good of the land; 20 but if you refuse and rebel, you shall be eaten by the sword; for the mouth of the LORD has spoken."*

God so patiently gives us a choice in every dilemma we face in life. We can choose between good and evil, right and wrong, and blessings and curses. Therefore, our choice has to be wisdom. We are winners, even when our circumstances do not agree. I know my circumstances often didn't agree, but I still gave God praise and thanks. As a result, I watched God remove barriers and distractions that would have taken me away from victory in an area of my life.

Thanksgiving is your primary weapon in the midst of affliction and frustration, but that weapon must be chosen in the time of battle. One key fact about giving God thanks is that when we begin to be thankful by faith, we release God's grace in our lives. The Apostle Paul tells us our status before and after salvation in Romans 3:23-24.

> *Romans 3:23-24 (ESV) for all have sinned and fall short of the glory of God, 24 and are justified by his grace as a gift, through the redemption that is in Christ Jesus,*

The grace of God is His willingness to get involved in our situations. In order to really win in the Kingdom of God, we must allow God to enter our lives and help us work through the situation we face. What I do know and understand is that we all have a choice. I can choose to look at the past with anger and regret or focus on the present with faith and expectation. We can murmur and complain, or we can trust and obey God. One key fact about murmuring and complaining is that it's evil in God's sight. Thousands of Israelites died in the wilderness because of their murmuring and complaining.

> *Numbers 16:41-49 (ESV) But on the next day all the congregation of the people of Israel grumbled against Moses and against Aaron,*

saying, "You have killed the people of the
LORD." 42 And when the congregation had
assembled against Moses and against Aaron,
they turned toward the tent of meeting. And
behold, the cloud covered it, and the glory of
the LORD appeared. 43 And Moses and Aaron
came to the front of the tent of meeting, 44 and
the LORD spoke to Moses, saying, 45 "Get
away from the midst of this congregation, that I
may consume them in a moment." And they fell
on their faces. 46 And Moses said to Aaron,
"Take your censer, and put fire on it from off
the altar and lay incense on it and carry it
quickly to the congregation and make
atonement for them, for wrath has gone out
from the LORD; the plague has begun." 47 So
Aaron took it as Moses said and ran into the
midst of the assembly. And behold, the plague
had already begun among the people. And he
put on the incense and made atonement for
the people. 48 And he stood between the dead
and the living, and the plague was stopped. 49
Now those who died in the plague were
14,700, besides those who died in the affair of
Korah.

I believe that everybody has something to
complain about. Being a winner and having a
winning mentality will not allow you to complain. It
is not easy to accept that we will have to endure
trouble. Often times we run from battles because
battles can be uncomfortable. However, for
Christians, our victory is assured. If we want to win

every time, we must understand that God is the source of our victories and successes.

> *Psalms 28:6-8 (ESV) Blessed be the LORD! For he has heard the voice of my pleas for mercy. 7 The LORD is my strength and my shield; in him my heart trusts, and I am helped; my heart exults, and with my song I give thanks to him. 8 The LORD is the strength of his people; he is the saving refuge of his anointed.*

The Apostle Paul tells us in 2 Corinthians 2:14 that God is our source of triumph.

> *2 Corinthians 2:14 (ESV) But thanks be to God, who in Christ always leads us in triumphal procession, and through us spreads the fragrance of the knowledge of him everywhere.*

As winners, we should recognize that our faith is the victory that conquers the world, sickness, poverty, bondage, and pressure. We need faith to win every battle, and faith will bring kingdom results. Faith is a practical expression of your confidence in God and His Word. Every attack in life is an attack on your faithfulness. The enemy knows that if he can persuade us to operate in fear rather than faith, we will abort the wonderful destiny the Father has planned for us. You will not have to endure anything God has not already empowered you to go through.

Your victory is already established because of that victory at the Cross that we talked about in chapter nine.

If we believe we are winners, here are some things that I know we must practice every day. First, it is crucial to stay in the Word. You will know the truth (or the Word), and it will set you free.

> *John 8:31-32 (ESV) So Jesus said to the Jews who had believed him, "If you abide in my word, you are truly my disciples, 32 and you will know the truth, and the truth will set you free."*

Your freedom only comes from the revelation you receive from the truth you know. Revelation knowledge is the knowledge God reveals to us through His word. See, the devil cannot suggest that you believe his lies when you are in God's Word and receiving revelation from the Father. Always remember that the first degree of truth is written in God's Word. God will always speak through His Word. God begins to speak when you are in the Word, and that Word gets in you. When those prophetic words from God begin to flow in your life, you will experience breakthrough after breakthrough.

If I am ever going to experience the Word of God, I have to be in it so that I will begin to experience the voice behind it. Winners in the Kingdom of God spend time in the Word of God because that brings the voice of God, and the voice of

God brings solutions to your life. The devil wants you never to read the written Word because he knows if you do, that will heal your body and set you free! Hallelujah!

> *Psalms 107:19-21 (ESV) Then they cried to the LORD in their trouble, and he delivered them from their distress. 20 He sent out his word and healed them, and delivered them from their destruction. 21 Let them thank the LORD for his steadfast love, for his wondrous works to the children of man!*

We are saved from destruction because of the Word! The Word saved us and brought us to a place called victory! I am so grateful that Jesus chose you and me for greatness and made us winners. When I consider the losses in my life, I cannot help but recognize the wins Christ brought to my life! I can only repeat what the Apostles Paul said, "What then shall we say to these things? If God is for us, who can be against us?"

> *Romans 8:31-39 (ESV) What then shall we say to these things? If God is for us, who can be against us? 32 He who did not spare his own Son but gave him up for us all, how will he not also with him graciously give us all things? 33 Who shall bring any charge against God's elect? It is God who justifies. 34 Who is to condemn? Christ Jesus is the one who died— more than that, who was raised—who is at the*

right hand of God, who indeed is interceding for us. 35 Who shall separate us from the love of Christ? Shall tribulation, or distress, or persecution, or famine, or nakedness, or danger, or sword? 36 As it is written, "For your sake we are being killed all the day long; we are regarded as sheep to be slaughtered." 37 No, in all these things we are more than conquerors through him who loved us. 38 For I am sure that neither death nor life, nor angels nor rulers, nor things present nor things to come, nor powers, 39 nor height nor depth, nor anything else in all creation, will be able to separate us from the love of God in Christ Jesus our Lord.

We are winners in Christ, and when we seek Him, we find Him. When we stay in the Word of God, we receive a Word from God. When we receive a Word from God, we begin to understand the type of person we have become is more important to God than successes and failures.

We can all try fame, money, and love, but we will be back because fulfillment is in the Word of God. I have been doing the right thing in the wrong place with the wrong people, and that never brought happiness or fulfillment to my life.

The Father has a plan for us. However, we will only experience that victorious life when we decide to win with the Word of God. Be the winner you were destined to be!! Beloved, we have what it takes!

Winning The War In Your Mind-
YOU HAVE WHAT IT TAKES!

NOTES
WINNING THE WAR IN YOUR MIND
YOU HAVE WHAT IT TAKES

NOTES
WINNING THE WAR IN YOUR MIND
YOU HAVE WHAT IT TAKES

NOTES
WINNING THE WAR IN YOUR MIND
YOU HAVE WHAT IT TAKES

NOTES
WINNING THE WAR IN YOUR MIND
YOU HAVE WHAT IT TAKES

NOTES
WINNING THE WAR IN YOUR MIND
YOU HAVE WHAT IT TAKES

ABOUT THE AUTHOR

Shannon Frazier was born on March 29, 1973, to Peggye and Herman Frazier and was raised in Greensboro, North Carolina. He had a natural ability to play music because his father, grandfather, uncles, and aunt were all church musicians. At the young age of seven, he began to play the drums for New Calvary Baptist Church, where the former Pastor Curtis Carrington was overseer. Shannon excelled on the drums, and by age twelve, he was introduced to the piano by his father, who gave him his first piano lesson. He started to play the piano and organ for the church and became the assistant to his mother, the choir director of the "Junior Choir."

He grew up with loving parents who openly displayed the love of God in their lives, and he grew a passion and love for God. This passion would explain why his life changed tremendously at age thirteen. Shannon knew at a young age that God was real and that Jesus loved him, and on July 7, 1985, he was baptized in front of many witnesses and family.

Shannon was well on his way to impact the world and did not have a clue as to what God was going to do with him. By age fifteen, he had an opportunity to play for the gospel legend "Shirley Caesar" when she came to town at St. Thomas Chapel Pentecostal Holiness Church which was a game-changing moment in his ministry and career. Shannon continued to serve faithfully with his parents at church until age eighteen. He left home for the first time and headed to North Carolina Central University in Durham, N.C., where he studied criminal justice and Music Education.

After three years of school, Shannon had an opportunity to travel and play the organ and piano for several evangelists, pastors, and Stage Plays. He began to see the world. His first stop was St. Kitts, Nevis, where Shannon was the crusade musician, after which he landed the "Sister Act Musical," which toured Italy, Switzerland, Germany, The British Virgin Islands, Jamaica, and Puerto Rico.

After returning to Greensboro, North Carolina, he decided to move to Houston, Texas. He was introduced to Lakewood Church and began to play as lead organist and assisted with the young adult service named "Portico." He later became the Music Director for a youth group in Houston called (Global Force), and with that group, they shared the stage with artists like Jason Crab, Israel Houghton, New Breed, and many others. He also recorded a live video with Donna Richardson-Joyner called "Sweating In The Spirit," which included Gospel artists Rizen, Myron Butler, Martha Munizzi, and Byron Cage. Shannon met the anointed Dr. Cindy Trimm and began to tour Zimbabwe and Johannesburg, South Africa. He visited Bishop Tudor Bismarck's church in Zimbabwe and later began to assist Bishop with the organ when he came to Houston, Texas.

Shannon knew that God was moving in his life, but he also knew God wanted and needed more from him. In 2005 he answered the call of God to preach the Word! He began to study and seek God's direction. Shannon started a small Friday night Bible Study called "Connect" on the east side of Houston T.X., where God impacted the community. That ministry was able to feed over 100 women and children diagnosed and affected with HIV in November 2007 for thanksgiving. Later in 2009, he accepted the position of Associate Pastor of Worship & Arts at a local church in Houston, where he exercised his ability to teach God's Word on Sunday mornings and Bible Study nights.

The Father has Blessed Shannon with experience, but more importantly, he has received the baptism with the Holy Spirit and operates with God's anointed power. Shannon is currently the lead Pastor of Abiding Faith Church of Baytown, Texas. He has served faithfully at Abiding Faith and continues to build a legacy in the city of Baytown, Texas. He has received revelation knowledge from God, which has made his teachings on the Word of God very practical and motivating. Many lives have been changed because of the passion and anointing that he speaks with. He is now traveling throughout the country, spreading the Word of God by teaching people life principles and displaying God's incredible love and power. He is married to Shanel Frazier and has two handsome sons, Seth and Josiah. Shannon has been called to encourage the discouraged and the lost and bring them to Jesus Christ.

Made in the USA
Coppell, TX
16 March 2023

14306413R00049